The l

bachelor's

cookbook©

First published in 2002 by Rathcline Publications, 4 Dodder Court,
Dundrum Road, Milltown, Dublin 14, Ireland.

ISBN 0-9544136-0-1

Words and design by Stephen Conmy
Typeset by Rathcline Publications
Printed in Ireland by W & G Baird Ltd.

While every care has been taken in the compilation of 'The Irish
bachelor's cookbook', neither the writer or the publishers can accept
responsibility for errors or omissions.

Stephen Conmy is editor of ShelfLife magazine, a
contributor to Wine Ireland magazine and a
freelance writer. He would like to thank Bronagh
Hayden, John Doyle, Doreen Kennedy, Jacinta
Delahaye, Kate Slattery, Pat Austin, Dermot
O'Connor, and his family and friends for their
encouragement and support.

THIS MENU WASN'T WRITTEN BY A COOK – IT WAS PUT DOWN BY A MAN

So you've left the mammy? Or else the missus left you?

Is your idea of cooking a hot meal beans on toast or microwaved chicken wings?

Well, relax. This little book is idiot proof. You need nothing fancy. If you can't find everything you need for the menu in your local supermarket then it's a crap shop.

You'll need a couple of pots and a wooden spoon, and a cooker. Knives will also help, although if you're really rough you can still use your fingers.

We even recommend the beer and wine and sauces to suit the menu. And if your guilty conscience is really bugging you, we have a few dishes that will impress the womenfolk.

What's more, our menu is fairly healthy. Well it's a lot healthier than doing take away or carvery every day, so your flabby gut won't get out of control.

T H E

HOME COOKIN'

* The fry

* Steak

* Lamb chops

* Pork chops

* Perfect Salmon steaks (oven baked in tin foil)

* Best omelette in the world

* Mammy's Irish stew cooked by you

* A casserole – beef, lamb, chicken ... whatever

* White fish – brain food

* A great salad – easy and will impress the bird

M E N U

FOREIGN FARE

* Spag Bol

* Chicken curry

* Red curry

* Green curry

* Fried rice

* Chicken pesto

* Chilli to die for

* Healthy Chinese vegetarian job

* Shrimp chow mein

* The ultimate Indian

SO YOU'RE ON YOUR OWN IN THE BIG BAD WORLD?

First things first – cooking is as simple as farting, why do you think all the world's top chefs are men?

Processed foods and take-aways are as healthy as cigs & booze sessions.

It's high time you learned how easy it is to cook up good honest fare.

Most of these dishes will not take longer than 20 minutes to cook. Some only take a few minutes.

Forget the microwave.

A man is never alone in the kitchen – he is making love to his stomach!

SAYING GOODBYE TO MAMMY CAN BE HARD

But there are benefits to leaving mammy, and cooking for yourself:
* You'll get a greater sense of independence
* You'll become more creative
* Supermarkets won't frighten you anymore
* You can impress mates with your new collection of pots and pans
* Ordering take-away will become a treat
* You can impress the ladies with salads and stuff
* You'll control your weight better
* You'll save loads of cash
* You'll make your mammy proud

(What you learn over the next few pages will also come in handy if you eventually get hitched to a girl who thinks it's okay to boil eggs in a kettle)

SAY 'BYE BYE MAMMY'

THE FRY

Ah yes, the good old heart-stopper. Fantastic on a Sunday morning after a few pints the night before. Try not to stuff these into you every morning, but the odd one will do you more good than harm. If you're not enjoying life, you're not living.

STUFF YOU'LL NEED

Eggs

Sausages

Rashers

Black pudding

Beans

Tomatoes

Mushrooms

Brown bread

Butter, Salt & pepper, Olive oil

Red & brown sauce, and Tobasco

GET TO IT

Bang on the pan at just above medium heat. Slap on a nice bit of olive oil.

Make sure it's hot (stick a sausage in and see if it sizzles) and then chuck in your meat – two rashers, two sausages , four slices of pud.

The key to a fry is to keep your eye on what's going on with the meat. Stand over it, don't piss-off and watch the telly. Using your wooden spoon, or spatula (a great word that!), keep the meat turning, so it browns rather than burns.

Stick on your beans, keeping them at low heat so they don't stick to the pot.

When the meat is nearly done chuck in your mushrooms and tomatoes. Make sure they're cut up into the size you want.

Keep the meat and veg going for a couple of minutes. Now stick the brown bread into the toaster.

Pop the meat and veg onto a nice big plate along with the beans. Put the pan back on, add a little more oil, and then crack your egg in a swift movement, dumping the contents into the middle of the pan.

The secret to a good fried egg is to let the bottom get hard before you try and turn it. Or just don't turn it.

Get the grub all together, butter up the toast, pour yourself a mug of tea and sit down.

Before eating, flavour the food with whatever you like.

THE STEAK

If a man can't cook a steak then he might as well throw the towel in.
Irish beef is the best in the world. Your local butcher will always have a
good selection of steaks. All you have to do is ask him for "a nice bit of
steak". He'll know what you mean and will hold up various pieces of
mouth-watering red flesh until you give him the nod. Ask for Sirloin or
Striploin. If you fancy a good chew ask for T-bone.

THE STUFF

A nice bit of steak from the butchers (you choose how big and fat it is)

Four rooster spuds, each the size of a cue ball

A nice fist-sized clump of broccoli

A few sticks of celery

A medium-sized onion

A handful of button mushrooms

A small glass of beer or red wine

Olive oil

Freshly-ground black pepper

Salt

Whatever sauce from a bottle you like

GET TO IT

Put on the spuds first. Roosters are great 'cos they cook well, are nearly always fluffy and taste super. Cover 'em with water in a pot and whack 'em on at full heat.

In fifteen minutes pop on the pan at just above medium heat. Slap on a bit of oil.

When its hot, bung in your steak. Brown one side and then the next.

Turn down the heat and keep turning it every two minutes. Pour a bit of wine or beer on it. Not too much though.

Now chop your onion into rings, and rinse the mushrooms, and then throw them onto the pan.

Now chop the celery, get the broccoli into nice-sized bits and throw them into the same pot as the spuds.

If you want a bloody steak take it off after five minutes. You can cut into it with a knife to check out how it looks in the middle.

Check the spuds with a knife after twenty minutes. If it slides through easily, they're done, along with the celery and broccoli. Strain them. Put 'em on a plate, add the steak and onions and mushrooms. Bingo!

LAMB CHOPS

There's nothing as tasty as a few nice lamb chops, some spuds and a nice pile of mashed turnip, all set up with a dollop of brown sauce. Me feckin' mouth is waterin' already! Lamb chops will take about ten to fifteen minutes to cook, so stick the spuds and turnip on first. The trick with the turnip is to cut half a head into smallish chunks (matchbox size) and boil them until they are soft. Use separate pots for the spuds and turnip.

STUFF YOU'LL NEED

Two or three nice gigot lamb chops. You'll know the right ones when the butcher shows 'em to you. The less fat the better.

Four nice cue-ball sized roosters (see page 50)

Half of a nice firm turnip, cut up into lumps

Olive oil

Salt & pepper

Brown sauce

GET TO IT

Put on the spuds (see page 50 for perfect spuds).

Chop up the turnip and cover the pieces with water. Put them on a high heat until they boil and then turn the heat down and let them simmer. Like spuds, turnip is done when you can slide a knife threw the pieces easily.

Ten minutes later, stick on the pan, oil her up, wait for her to heat and then throw on the lamb chops. Keep the heat fairly high to medium.

Just keep an eye on the chops by turning them every two minutes. They should be done in less than ten. If they start burning, take 'em off.

When your spuds are done, drain them and let them rest in the pot while you take care of the turnip.

Strain the turnip pieces. Put them back in the same empty pot and add a bit of butter and salt and pepper, and then mash the hell out of 'em until you get a nice pot of mashed turnip.

Put the spuds and chops and turnips on a plate, sit down and pour on the brown sauce.

The ultimate Monday night dinner!

An ice-cold glass of proper milk is yer only man for this type of fare.

PORK CHOPS

As the great man Homer J. once said, you can't have pork chops without apple sauce. Well, actually you can. If you want the apple flavour, get hold of a nice Granny Smith, peel it, and then, using your peeler, shave the flesh of the apple. Pork chops go great with sweet corn, oven chips, and a helping of beans. This is real honest grub – mouth-watering and simple. Should take minutes to prepare and seconds to devour.

THE STUFF

Two nice pork chops. Your butcher will help you out if you ask for two nice ones, not too thick.

Oven chips – go for the medium ones.

Small tin of fresh young corn nibblets and a small tin of beans.

An apple, if you want the apple on the chops. Some don't like apple on pork chops so it's up to you.

Olive oil

Salt & pepper

Red & brown sauce

GET TO IT

Get an oven tray and lay down a sheet of tin foil on it. The tray is probably all grubby and dirty so instead of washing it the tin foil will do.

Spread a nice load of chips evenly over the tray and bang 'em in the oven at 200 degrees.

Five minutes later start frying your chops.

Splash of olive oil, medium/high heat on the knob, and chuck 'em on when it's hot enough.

It's important to cook pork properly, so overcook 'em rather than undercook 'em, the flavour gets better when they're nicely done.

When the chips are done, stick the plate in the oven while you heat up the corn and the beans.

Heat the corn and beans.

An ice-cold bottle of beer goes really well with this supper.

SALMON STEAKS IN TIN FOIL

There isn't an easier way to cook fish. You can use this method with any type of fish really – trout, cod, John Dory, whatever takes your fancy.

THE STUFF

Tin foil, about half a foot squares for each steak

Two salmon steaks, with or without bones

Six nice baby potatoes of equal size

Four stalks of asparagus

A big enough carrot

A lemon

A knob of butter

Bit of basil

Salt & pepper

Mayonnaise

GET TO IT

Grease up the tin foil squares with some olive oil or a bit of butter if you want. Place the salmon steaks in the middle of the squares. Squeeze lemon juice over them. Add salt and pepper and stick a few basil leaves on top of them.

Wrap them up into little parcels, but not too tightly, you'll want them to breathe a little.

Stick 'em in the oven, at the top, at 180 degrees for twenty minutes.

Bang on the spuds. These should take no longer than twenty minutes either. Remember, if the knife slides in you're winning.

Steam the asparagus over the boiling spuds by putting them in a strainer and putting the strainer over the boiling pot. Cover the strainer with the lid of the pot. This will save you using another pot for veggies. (* See page 50 for further tips).

Do the carrots in the same strainer as the asparagus. Chop them in thin slices, and keep them a little crunchy by not steaming them for too long.

The salmon steaks will be cooked when the flesh gets very light pink and the skin comes off real easy.

Whack all your good stuff onto a plate. Slap a blob of mayo beside your fish and Bob's yer uncle. A posh bit of nosh but as simple as putting the ball in an empty net from five yards.

Squeeze some more lemon over the fish if you like that sort of thing.

BEST OMELETTE IN THE WORLD

This is without doubt one of the easiest and tastiest things you can rustle up in minutes. It's dead cheap as well. Eggs are good if you work out with weights regularly, but not that good for you if you're a fat arse who sits watching telly and swallowing cans all evening. So be the judge of how often you eat these yourself.

STUFF YOU'LL NEED

Four free-range eggs

A splash of milk, a little butter, and a half hand-full of grated cheddar cheese

Five or six mushrooms

A tomato

Two slices of ham

Three scallions

Olive oil

Salt & pepper

GET TO IT

This is so easy to make. Just get a large bowl. Crack your eggs into it.

Now add a splash of milk and a little butter and beat the eggs, real good.

Then chop up your mushrooms, scallions, tomato and ham into little pieces.

Throw them all into the bowl and mix 'em all up.

Bang on a frying pan at medium heat, add the oil. When it's hot just pour the contents of the bowl onto the pan.

Sprinkle the cheese onto the omelette, and turn on the grill of your oven to number four.

After five minutes or so, take the pan off the knob and put it under the grill.

Leave there for five minutes.

You'll know when it's done when you see the cheese getting all melted and a little crusty, or just cut into it and have a little taste. Just keep an eye on it.

Get the salt and pepper onto it, sit down and enjoy it with some nice buttered brown bread.

MAMMY'S IRISH STEW
COOKED BY YOU

This is a brown stew, which is bloody tasty, and is dead easy to throw together. It takes a while to cook, but it's worth it. Ask your butcher for a half pound of lean stewing steak. He'll cut it up for you. Once you have all your stuff in the pot, you have an hour and a half to do whatever you want while she stews away.

THE STUFF

Half a pound of lean stewing steak from the butcher

Two smallish spuds for the stew pot

Four nice spuds for the plate

A couple of medium sized onions

Two fairly big carrots

A packet of country stew powder mix

Olive oil

Salt & pepper

GET TO IT

Get a big pot and splash a bit of olive oil into her. Keep her on medium to high heat.

When she's hot chuck in your meat. Make sure the pieces are nice and handy.

Brown the meat for a few minutes and you can whack in a bit of wine to tenderise it and add flavour if you want to be fancy.

Now peel the two small spuds and cut 'em in half. Peel the carrots and chop them too. Do the same to the onion, but cut them into four.

Throw all this into the pot and then get your stew mixture ready. Usually each packet needs a pint glass of water. Read the instructions.

Throw that into your meat and veg. Bring to the boil and then turn it down really low, to mark one, cover it and leave stewing for an hour and a half. Make sure she's just bubbling away slightly.

In an hour or so, bang on your spuds. When they're done in twenty minutes, peel 'em, get them onto a plate, cut em up, butter and salt 'em and then pour a nice helping of stew over them.

The best fuel to get into you before Saturday night pints!

A CASSEROLE – BEEF, CHICKEN, LAMB ... WHATEVER

A casserole is a bit like a stew except that you cook it in the oven and you can use chicken or beef or lamb, or all three if you want. The choice of meat is up to you. Casseroles are another tasty little number for those cold winter evenings. More of a weekend dish 'cos of the time it takes to cook. But they're so easy, basically you can be inventive and chuck whatever you want into this dish.

THE STUFF

A big casserole dish

Three quarters of a pound of whatever meat you want, from the butcher's and cut into nice mouth-size bits

(Any hard veg you want, but here's a few suggestions)

A nice-sized onion

A scattering of mushroom

A green pepper

Some celery stalks

Two juicy carrots

A couple of small spuds for the casserole pot

Four boiled spuds for your plate (see page 50)

A casserole packet

Salt & pepper

GET TO IT

Brown your meat a little by frying it up in some olive oil. Strain and bung it into your casserole dish.

Chop up your veg and two small spuds into nice little bits and throw them into the pot.

Whack in a good bit of black pepper.

The casserole packet usually needs a pint of water. Mix it up well and pour over the stuff in the casserole pot.

Cover the pot and stick it in the oven at around one-eighty (180 degrees). Leave her there for just over an hour.

With twenty minutes to go, do your spuds (see page 50).

Serve the whole lot up in a nice big bowl and get stuck in.

Great for a Sunday evening hangover with a nice bottle of vino.

WHITE FISH – BRAIN FOOD

For this dish you'll need to go to a fishmongers and ask for a nice bit of John Dory or monkfish. These tasty white-fleshed fish are great to cook, sturdy and have firm texture, and they're caught off Irish coasts so they'll be as fresh as daisies. Cook a few new baby spuds, a bit of broccoli and maybe a bit of cauliflower. For a great sauce, melt a little butter in a small pot and fry up some diced shallots (tiny little onions). White fish is great for the auld brain.

THE STUFF

A couple of nice lumps of John Dory or monkfish from the monger

Four new baby spuds

A nice clump of broccoli and a bit of cauliflower (as much as you think you'd eat)

Two shallots

Some butter

A sprig of parsley

Salt & pepper

GET TO IT

Wrap the fish in tin foil parcels with the parsley and some salt & pepper.

Bang 'em in the oven for twenty minutes or so at
one hundred & eighty degrees.

Stick on your spuds and cook until they're done (see page 50).

You can steam the broccoli and cauliflower in a strainer on top of the
spud pot for ten minutes. It'll save you using another pot.

Melt butter in a pot, dice up your shallots, chuck 'em in and fry them
for a minute. Add a little more butter so it's all melted and nice.

The fish will be done when the flesh is nice and stiff in about twenty
minutes. Keep your eye on it.

Pop the fish and the spuds and the veg onto a plate and pour your butter
& shallot sauce over them.

If you're into the auld religion, then this meal is good for Fridays! It's a
myth that dogs don't like fish. She's just eaten a crab!

A GREAT SALAD – EASY AND WILL IMPRESS THE BIRD

You'd be surprised how easy it is to toss up a great-looking and tasty salad in a few seconds, and if you're trying to impress a lady friend then she'll be grateful that you can do something other than order chips and heat some beans. You can buy whatever dressing you want – Italian, French, Vinaigrette, or whatever. Here you learn how to make your own. Get a big bowl and get tossing.

THE STUFF

Iceberg lettuce

Endive and Cos lettuce

Cherry tomatoes

Cucumber

Scallions

Feta cheese (or little bits of any cheese type you like)

A yellow pepper

2 mushrooms

Salad dressing (a spoon of Irish hot mustard, one shot glass of cider vinegar and three shot glasses of olive oil)

Black pepper

GET TO IT

Chop up the lettuce roughly.

Chop up all the other veg into tiny little pieces, the smaller the better.

Throw everything into a big bowl along with the cheese bits.

Sprinkle a bit of pepper on.

To make a dressing put the mustard, the oil and the cider vinegar into a cup and mix it like hell.

Pour some dressing over the salad and toss it with a fork.

Healthy, nutritious and will impress the ladies!

FOREIGN FARE

Foreign dishes might sound exotic and taste great when you get them in a restaurant or a take-away. But you can actually do them better yourself, and they're dead easy to cook. Basically, most of them take twenty minutes to cook up, and most of them go with rice, which is dead handy.

Curries and the like are really just fancy stews. They're just a little more spicy. Most of these meals go great with beer. Once you've done a few you'll be a dab hand at fancy dishes.

For most of these dinners, all you'll need is two pots to cook in. Simple.

SPAG BOL

Ah yes, the height of sophisticated continental eating in the 80s – good old Spaghetti Bolognese. The auld Spag Bol is a winner any day of the week. It's so easy to make it's pathetic. You can always buy a jar but here we show you how to make your own tasty sauce. Simple!

THE STUFF

Half a pound of lean mince from the butcher

A tin of chopped tomatoes with basil, or a tin of plum tomatoes

An onion

A clove of garlic

Olive oil

A shot glass of red wine

A spoon of Irish mustard

A spoon of sugar

Pasta (any shape you want)

Grated cheese (any kind you like)

Salt & pepper

GET TO IT

First the sauce. Dice the onion and fry it along with the chopped garlic in a pot using olive oil for a minute. Throw the tin of tomatoes into the pot and make sure they're all mushed up. Bring to the boil, then turn the heat down so it's just bubbling lightly.

Add the spoon of mustard and the spoon of sugar to the mix. Throw in the red wine. Leave simmering for about twenty minutes.

In the mean time, stick on your pasta (see page 51 for the perfect pasta).

Brown your mince too. This should take five minutes and when it's done, you can pour some of the sauce over the meat and let it bubble away nicely for ten minutes or so until the pasta is done.

When it's all on the plate lookin' great, sprinkle on a good dose of grated cheese. One mouthful and you'll think you can open up your own Italian joint!

CHICKEN CURRY

Curries are like stews. They're all about getting meat and veg, covering them with a sauce, allowing them to boil away for a while and then eating them with some form of starchy food like spuds, or rice or chips. Curries are dead easy to make.

THE STUFF

A nice firm breast of chicken

An onion

Two stalks of celery

Half a red pepper

A packet of curry powder (hot or mild, you choose)

A dose of long grain rice (see page 51 for the perfect rice)

Olive oil

Salt & pepper

GET TO IT

Chop up the chicken and the onion, get your pan or pot going with the oil and when it's hot, throw in your onion, sizzle 'em for a minute and then add your chicken pieces.

Fry them up at medium heat until the chicken is white and then add your chopped up celery and half a red pepper diced.

Now sprinkle on your curry powder from the packet. Add the water, bring to the boil and then turn the heat down and let it bubble away gently.

Now slap on your rice (see page 51 for the perfect rice).

Serve it all up and enjoy with a nice crisp, cool beer. Tasty bird, eh? Magic!

RED CURRY

Thai food is nearly as popular as the auld Chinese grub, so here's how to cook up the famous Thai curries. They're dead easy to do. You can choose whatever meat you want to go with the sauce. Here, we are doing a red beef curry. Red and green curry pastes are in any good shop, and don't worry, even restaurants use these pastes.

THE STUFF

Get some beef, cut by the butcher into stir fry sized pieces. He'll do it for you in a jiffy

Red curry paste

A tin of coconut milk

A yellow pepper

Three green scallions

A red or green chilli (make sure you take out the seeds unless you want to blow your mouth off)

Half a cup of frozen peas or some mangetout

A mug full of Basmati rice

GET TO IT

Fry your beef with some olive oil in a pot. You can throw a bit of beer in to tenderise it and add flavour if you like. When the meat is nicely cooked, strain off the juices.

Now add three tablespoons of red curry paste and fry the beef at medium heat for a minute or so.

Throw in your chopped scallions, and chopped pepper, and chopped chilli and peas and mix them all up so the paste covers them. Fry for thirty seconds or so.

Now chuck in your tin of coconut milk. Bring to the boil and then reduce heat so it's bubbling away softly.

It'll be ready in thirty minutes, so put on your rice with ten minutes to go (See page 51).

True Thai flavours in your own kitchen. And you thought it would be difficult!

GREEN CURRY

This is the more popular Thai curry. It can be vegetarian but here we are going to cook a green chicken curry. A good green paste and nice coconut milk are essential for success.

THE STUFF

A lovely big pert breast of chicken

Green curry paste

A tin of coconut milk

A yellow pepper

Three green scallions

A red or green chilli (make sure you take out the seeds unless you want to blow your mouth off)

Half a cup of frozen peas or some mangetout

A mug full of Basmati rice

(If you want the veggie version, just don't add the chicken, throw in a few chopped-up spuds instead)

GET TO IT

In a pot, fry up your diced chicken breast in some olive oil at medium heat. When it's white and dry it's cooked.

Now add three tablespoons of green curry paste and fry the chicken at medium heat for a minute or so.

Throw in your chopped scallions, and chopped pepper, and chopped chilli and peas and mix them all up so the paste covers them. Fry for thirty seconds or so.

Now chuck in your tin of coconut milk. Bring to the boil and then reduce heat so it's bubbling away softly.

It'll be ready in thirty minutes, so put on your rice with ten minutes to go (See page 51).

True Thai flavours in your own kitchen. Did you notice that I took a short cut writing down this recipe? Brilliant!

FRIED RICE

This is a bloody tasty dish, on its own or as an accompaniment to curries, or fish or whatever. You can make your own fried rice and add anything you want to it – shrimp, ham, cooked chicken, left over turkey, or even cold roast beef. The secret to fried rice is the egg, and stirring it constantly while it fries on the pan. Here we're making plain fried rice with onion.

THE STUFF

A plate of cold, cooked rice

A medium onion

An egg

Olive oil

Salt & pepper

(Here's something to look at while you wait for the rice to get cold)

GET TO IT

Boil your rice (see page 51) and let it cool down by spreading it on a plate. It'll be cold enough in fifteen minutes.

Get your pan and put a good bit of olive oil on. Heat her up and then add your finely chopped onion.

Fry the onion for a minute and then start gradually adding the rice.

Now for the magic bit.

Crack an egg into a cup, whisk it and then pour the beaten egg over the rice in the pan.

Give it a good stir. The egg will stop the rice from sticking too much to the pan and fluff it up a bit.

Fry it all for about five minutes and then sit down and enjoy it with lots of salt & pepper.

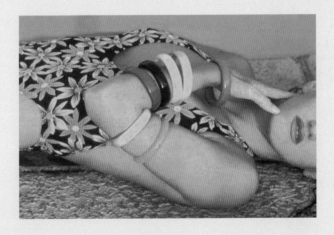

CHICKEN PESTO

This is a dead handy dish. It's tasty and not too filling. Perfect for summer afternoons, and will impress the ladies too. This is basically a chicken and pasta dish, but the green pesto really sets it off. You don't have to use too much pesto because it has a fairly strong flavour. The thinner the spaghetti the better, for this dish.

THE STUFF

A pert pink breast of chicken

A large spoon of green pesto

Some thin spaghetti

Five cherry tomatoes

Three scallions

Half a yellow pepper

Salt & pepper

Some French bread

GET TO IT

Cut up your breast of chicken into little pieces and fry them in olive oil until they are cooked thoroughly.

Boil up your spaghetti (see page 51).

Chop up your cherry tomatoes in half, and dice your yellow pepper and scallions.

When the pasta is cooked, strain it and then put it back in the same pot.

Add your chicken and the chopped goodies. Now whack in a nice big spoon of pesto and get stirring.

Sit down and enjoy with a nice cheeky white wine and some French bread. Very Euro-friendly I must say!

CHILLI TO DIE FOR

This brown baby will blow the hole off you! Only messin'. Chilli is no bother to rustle up. I mean, if cowboys can cook this then anyone can. You can make chilli as hot as you want. If you want a really hot one, leave the seeds in the red chilli. TABASCO sauce and chilli powder can also add extra spice if you want, 'cos the packet can be a bit bland for some people.

THE STUFF

Three quarters of a pound of nice lean mince

A packet of chilli con carne mix

A spoon of chilli powder

A red chilli

TABASCO sauce (see page 56)

A cup full of red kidney beans

A big onion

Some mushrooms

A tin of chopped tomatoes

Long grain rice (see page 51)

GET TO IT

Brown the mince in a pot with olive oil and add the finely chopped onion.

Now add the red chilli, finely chopped (remove the seeds if you don't want the burn), and the chopped mushrooms and red kidney beans.

Chuck in your spoon of chilli powder and the contents of the chilli con carne packet.

Add half a pint of water and the tin of tomatoes.

Slap in a good few squirts of TABASCO sauce.

Bring to the boil and leave to simmer gently for twenty minutes.

Serve with rice (page 51) and a nice cool beer, Staropramen is perfect.

Sit back and wait to see what noises you'll make!

HEALTHY CHINESE
VEGETARIAN JOB

This is really just a stir fry, but with the right veg, it looks great and tastes fantastic, plus it's dead healthy. So if you're feeling a little guilty about the last couple of weeks and the amount of beer you consumed, get one of these into you. It'll make you feel like a young slip of a thing again! You can throw whatever veg you want into this. Here we give a few suggestions.

THE STUFF

TIKKAMEN Soy sauce

Black pepper

Five fresh radishes

Three scallions

Three celery stalks

Five cherry tomatoes

A carrot, sliced really thin

A small courgette sliced really thin

A couple of chopped fresh mushrooms

Some 'baby corn', if not then a couple of spoons of tinned sweet corn

Rice, or new baby potatoes

GET TO IT

Janey this is so easy to cook!

Just chop up all your veg real nice, into nice small bits.

Do your rice or spuds first 'cos the veg will only take a couple of minutes (see page 51).

If you have a wok then great, if you don't, a frying pan will do.

Grease up the wok with olive oil and bang on the veg bit by bit. Using your wooden spoon, stir it and fry it.

Splash a bit of TIKKAMEN soy sauce all over the veg, as much or as little as you like. Fry it for a minute or so.

Serve on a plate of steaming rice or new spuds.

This'll remind you of Spring in the fields ... hmm!

SHRIMP CHOW MEIN

Chow Mein is on every Chinese menu and it's dead easy to make. It's the Chinese version of the Spag Bol! All it takes is getting some noodles going on the wok and throwing in some meat and veg and soy sauce. In this case we're gonna cook up some shrimps. Tasty little beggers that they are!

THE STUFF

A nice fist full of egg noodles

A handful of small pink shrimps

TIKKAMEN Soy sauce

Three scallions

Half a red pepper

A few water chestnuts

A handful of bamboo shoots

Veggie oil

GET TO IT

Cook up your dried egg noodles in a pot of boiling water. Should take about ten minutes. Test them before you strain them.

If you're using frozen shrimp, then boil them in salted water for seven minutes before you wok them.

Chop up your scallions and pepper.

When the noodles and shrimp are done, heat up your wok and add some vegetable oil.

Get it nice and hot, whack in your noodles, and then the shrimp and veggies and chestnuts and get stir frying.

The idea is to get the ingredients nice and hot, but not burnt.

During the stir frying, keep splashing on the TIKKAMEN soy sauce. As much as you feel you'd like, but five or six splashes won't do you any harm.

Serve with a cold crisp one, Beck's is spot on.

THE ULTIMATE INDIAN

This can be the dog's bollix if you get the right curry paste. A good Roghan Josh paste from the ethnic foods section of your local supermarket is better than most powders. To make a really good Indian, just keep your eye on it. Delicate touches may be required but don't expect the meal to be delicate with you! You can use chicken, lamb or beef. Here it's chicken.

THE ULTIMATE STUFF

A nice big, ripe, pink, firm breast of chicken

An onion

Three tablespoons of hot curry paste

Tin of crushed tomatoes

A green chilli pepper with seeds removed

Two, small, peeled spuds cut into mouth-size bits

A small yellow pepper

A mug of Basmatti rice

GET TO IT

Chop up the breast into nice mouth-size bits and fry them in a bit of oil at medium heat until they're white and cooked.

Chop up the onion into little bits and fry them up with the chicken. Then add the chopped peppers and chilli and bits of spud.

Now add three spoonfuls of the curry paste, mix in and fry the whole lot up for a minute at medium heat.

Now add the tin of tomatoes and bring to the boil. When it starts bubbling heavily, turn down the heat and let it simmer gently for half an hour.

With ten minutes to go, get your rice on (see page 51).

Serve this with an ice-cold bottle of crispy Staropramen beer.

Put the jaxx roll in the fridge!

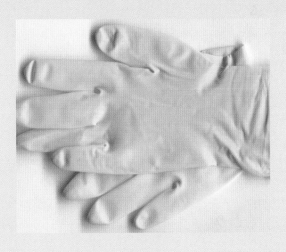

HANDY TIPS

HOW TO COOK PERFECT SPUDS, RICE AND PASTA

SPUDS

Spuds are simple just don't try and boil big ones. A perfect size of spud is about the diameter of the illustration below.

To boil good spuds, put them in a pot and cover them with water. Bring them to the boil and let them bubble away for twenty-five minutes. They're done when you can slide a knife easily through them, and their jackets should be slightly broken.

Rice

Loads of people say they can't 'do' good rice. It's easy, it takes a little bit of finesse that's all.

Basically the secret to nice fluffy rice is lots of boiling water. You can never have too much boiling water in your rice pot.

In a nice big pot of boiling water throw in your rice. A big mug full will normally do one person. Add a nice squirt of salt. And stir the rice immediately.

When it's boiling, turn the heat down so it's bubbling gently. Keep stirring. Stir it regularly. In ten minutes it should be nearly done. Take it off the boil. Cover it with a lid, and let it cook in its own steam. Check it every thirty seconds to see when it's at the perfect texture you like. Strain it and jazz it up with a fork. Bob's yer uncle, fluffy fantastic rice.

Pasta

Once again lads, loads of boiling water is great for good pasta. When the water is boiling, add a splash of olive oil to the water. This will prevent your pasta from sticking.

Don't cover pasta pots, let them boil away merrily but not violently. Have a boiled kettle on the stand by just in case the water levels drop dramatically.

Pasta should be done in twelve minutes. Take a bit out and check it. Like with rice, you can take it off the boil and let her cook in her own heat at the final stage.

DON'T BE AFRAID TO GET YOUR HANDS
HANDS
WET & SLIPPY

IT'LL BE WORTH IT IN THE
LONG RUN

WASHING UP

Let's you and me get slippery and wet baby! Washing up is a bit of a bore, but it's not a chore if you do it as you cook.

ALWAYS HAVE A SINK FULL OF WARM SOAPY WATER WHEN YOU ARE COOKING

When you finish with a knife or bowl or whatever, dump it in the sink to soak. When the pots are emptied of food, dunk them in the water. Keep water on everything, don't let oil and grease grind into pots, pans and dishes, making it really hard to wash 'em later.

Don't just rinse plates and cutlery under a running tap.
THIS DOESN'T CLEAN ANYTHING. A sink full of warm, soapy, slippy water is the only way forward.

THE BOOZE

BEER

Goes well with everything, from chips to peanuts. But did you know that beer is perfect for curries and spicy food 'cos it takes away some of the sting? If you want a few cool ones sitting pretty in the fridge, go for these bad boys.

Staropramen, Prague's number one lager, is a classic Czech pilsner with a full-rounded, well-balanced taste where hops dominates malt with a long lasting lacing foam. Great with curries and meat dishes.

A great beer. Has become popular with Irish beer drinkers, it's pure and tasty, and goes well with Thai food as well as pasta dishes.

'Without question, the greatest invention in the history of mankind is beer. Oh, I grant you that the wheel was also a fine invention, but the wheel does not go nearly as well with pizza.'
Dave Barry

Beck's is the most popular German beer in the world. Beck's is brewed in strict accordance with the "Reinheitsgebot", the German beer purity law of 1516, which stipulates that only four natural ingredients can be used in the brewing process: barley, hops, water and yeast. Beck's is best served at a temperature of between 4 – 6°C and is available in 500ml and 330ml bottles and non-alcoholic 330ml bottles.

Curim Gold from the Carlow Brewing Company is a great Summer drink and really quenches the thirst, so it stands to reason that it goes well with most dishes, especially curries.

THE WINE

'What contemptible scoundrel has stolen the cork to my lunch?'
W.C. Fields

If you're not big into wine then it's handy to know the basics. There's not much point in being able to waffle about wine at dinner parties unless you want to be known as the type of person who does that.

The basics of wine are simple. It should look good, smell good and taste good.

Wines are made from grapes and each grape has its own style, that's why you hear people saying things like "blackcurrant flavours" or "pepper and spice" or "gooseberry" and all that rubbish!
All you need to know is what style of wine you like and what food it goes well with. Here's four wines that are good entry-level drinkers, won't cost the earth, are available widely and have looks that will get the conversation going at any party.

Luna Di Luna is a range of wines suited for all tastes. As you can see the wines have brightly-coloured bottles with attractive labels. The wines themselves are blends, which means different grape varieties are used to make each one. The purple and red bottles contain red wine and the blue and green bottles contain white wine.

The so-called rule of thumb is that you should drink red wines with red meat and white wines with fish or chicken. Ignore this rule. It is old fashioned and snobbish. You should drink whatever wine you like with the meal you're enjoying. These four wines are a great place to start, or continue, your relationship with the good stuff! Enjoy.

Tasty!

Very tasty!

THE FLAVOUR

A good flavouring is the quick and easy key to cooking up really tasty nosh. Professional chefs use this stuff and so should you, and what's more it's completely affordable and can be found in all good shops. These two flavours will save you hours of time and give great results.

Kikkoman soy sauce is great for adding to anything that needs to be salted up a bit. Basically it gets the taste buds working over time and is great for Oriental dishes, and even as a replacement for salt.

Tobasco sauce is an essential for any bachelor – it gives deep and funky spices to everything and can be used as a replacement for pepper. Go easy though, if you're not used to it 'cos it really does have a lovely bite! This flavour is great with chilli, curries, and even adds spice to salads and baked beans. It's an all round spice provider.

THE COFFEE

Coffee is an essential end to any meal and to get real taste you have to drink real coffee. The Robt. Roberts Explorer range of coffees is ideal for any self-respecting bachelor. India, Australia and Ethiopia are the countries of origin for these coffees, so there's a real international flavour for you to enjoy. You might not think that Australia is a coffee growing country, well think again and try the Australian Skybury.

Notes

"Three things give us hardy strength: sleeping on hairy mattresses, breathing cold air, and eating dry food."
Welsh proverb

Notes

"The secret of staying young is to live honestly, eat slowly, and lie about your age."
Lucille Ball

NOTES

"Bachelor's fare: bread and cheese, and kisses."
Jonathan Swift, (1667-1745).

NOTES

"In cooking, as in all the arts, simplicity is the sign of perfection."
Curnonsky